Deliberately My Best at Sales

Deliberately My Best at Sales

Larry Wood, Expert

Contents

This book is dedicate to all those who *Deliberately want* to be their *Best* with communication in their professional and personal lives.

A special thank you to my family for their encouragement.

An acknowledgement to Greg and Pamela Smith Arnone for their insight and help with this book.

A tremendous amount of gratitude to Ron DuBois for his editing.

T HIS UNIQUE BOOK will teach you the sound science of selling. In these chapters, we will point out the inter-workings of which approach is best for a particular customer or market along with the "*best*" dialogue to use.

I will direct you onto a path of discovery where you will have the answer of whether that sale was just a coincidence or a predictable result. I guarantee your personal and professional abilities to communicate will **deliberately** be your **best** throughout the balance of your life after you have applied what is in this book.

WEDNESDAY AT NOON

IT IS NOON now and the meeting to close this deal is fifteen minutes over the time limit. The prospect is happy, still talking and I am thinking the "C" type communicator will lose track of time and we will never ink the deal. I want to close this one hundred thousand dollar software deal to make me number one.

Nelson, my prospect, takes a breath and I jump in with a comment, "this looks like you have created the "perfect-time to sign the contracts." Nelson said, "Larry, I have, where do I sign?" and "Oh, let me call for the check." The next event to take place was the proper amount of handshakes to everyone involved and then the big "WOW" moment from Nelson.

Nelson with a grin blurted out, "Larry, I feel as though you read my mind, everything in our conversation felt so good, so comfortable, like I just experienced mental sex with words and no vulgarity or suggestive language, if there is such a thing. How did this happen? Do I need to have a smoke or a drink now?"

At that moment, I was *deliberately* my *best*.

SELLING CHRISTMAS CARDS

I WAS NINE YEARS old and living in Ft. Lauderdale Florida, my hometown. It was an average suburban neighborhood with green lawns, fenced in yards and a local school the neighborhood kids could walk to together.

I would cut our family's lawn and my dad would give me twenty five cents on Saturday. Depending on what I wanted to spend my money on, that would decide whether I would walk the neighborhood and offer my services to cut other lawns for twenty five cents.

Typically on Saturday afternoons a group of my friends from the neighborhood would walk to PJ's Drug Store at NW 6th Avenue and Sunrise Boulevard to buy a root beer float at the lunch counter. To be able to afford that there had to be a plan, I knew the cost of the root beer float. With a gallon of Amoco gas for twenty-five cents, I would be able to cut ten plus yards. That would earn enough money for my afternoon delight.

Now this plan coupled with my positive attitude and charismatic personality I later learned would lead me to greater riches. My preparation was looking for opportunity. The adventure did rev-up my emotional engine which did transfer to the potential customer automatically. Being enthusiastic made it more fun. Little by little a pattern for selling was being created.

If the house I walked up to had a "groomed" yard like a fresh hair cut, I would go to the next yard. If it had that average look, this was a winner. This went on for a couple of years and really taught me a great deal about business and building relationships.

During this time, the sixties and seventies, my passion for music really grew and it was well nurtured. Every Saturday night my uncles, aunt and cousins would come over to our home for a barbeque. There would be a lot of music, singing and dancing late into the night.

When my parents saw all the fun I was having playing an air guitar and singing, they gave me a guitar with lessons. The guitar lessons were at Shoemaker's Music Store in downtown Ft. Lauderdale with Mrs. Griffin as the excellent and incredibly fun music teacher. The singing lessons came from the church choir.

The guitar had flames on it and it was great. But learning the "Yellow Rose of Texas" was just not enough speed for me. My father gave me an album of Chet Akins and my mother gave me an album of Jose Feliciano and they both said "learn to play like them."

To me this was powerful; to own an album with my favorite music and songs recorded on it. I could play it anytime and as much as I liked. But I wanted to be able to buy the albums of the artists and bands of my choice, which called for a plan.

So was reading a Life magazine and there was an offer to join the Columbia Record of the Month Club. They would automatically send the newest album from the genre of my choice every month. Man-a-live this is for me, I said out loud and so I joined after talking about it at the dinner table with my parents. A few weeks later the first album arrived. I would play my guitar and sing with the album. I thought this is "living large."

The problem was the cost of one album was a little more than I could earn cutting lawns in a month. The answer this time was in a Superman comic book that I was reading. There was an advertisement to sell Christmas cards. The offer explains the business plan which includes the selling process, order fulfillment and delivery of the product. Then there would be a commission check. All I could see was a plan that would work.

My father and I talked it over; it made good business sense so I agreed to work the plan. At that time selling door-to-door was an accepted and customary manner of conducting business. I remember to this day my mother having me translate (she is Cuban and her English is not perfect) for the Kirby vacuum salesman, World Book Encyclopedia and, our neighborhood Girl Scouts selling their cookies at our front door.

Finally the Christmas card catalog arrived at our home, it was very handsome. These cards were the best looking holiday cards my family had ever seen. The big bonus was the company would print your name in cursive inside the card with any color you wanted. I was thinking that I was on Easy Street and this was money in the bank.

So the plan was to sell to my already existing lawn service customers, friends from school, church and extended family members. With this plan the total commissions would equal one year's worth of albums from the Columbia Record Album of the month Club. I was prepared. I had the catalog, prices, customers and motivation. I expected everyone to appreciate my Christmas cards because they were so beautiful and could have that fancy signature in as well.

Selling after school was simple as everyone's mother was home and my first dozen orders really went pretty smoothly. It seemed like everybody was happy to talk about Christmas in late October or early November. I found myself repeating to each customer, "Wow look at that one, it is so beautiful."

I genuinely loved the product and it came across. The customer felt my passion and that triggered the same emotion from them. Sales were smoking hot! It was like I had a wand.

But at last I came to the door of one of my lawn customers and she said, "These cards are nice but it not personal when you don't sign yourself." I responded, "My parents can't read everyone's signature on the cards we receive. They have to guess who sent it. With the engraving it takes the guess work out of who sent these beautiful cards and it adds that holiday touch with your signature in gold". She made the purchase.

Unfortunately the sales catalog did not have a script for overcoming objections. Not being a professional trained salesperson at nine years old, my instincts lead me to re-establish the value of the unique features and benefits of what I saw in the cards to my customer.

Struggles to complete the sale were everywhere as I would canvas beyond my immediate neighborhood for a couple of blocks, these families really did not know me so it was a little tougher to close the sale, my passion was not always enough to put it in the bank.

What really helped were statements I remember my recently immigrated Cuban uncles, aunts and cousin would say at our home on Saturday nights. They would say, "Only in America can you do this," or "Anyone can earn money in America," and "This is a wonderful country. If you work hard in America you can earn money."

In reality, this family banter was an informal sales training guide for me. I took those positive comments along with the patriotic enthusiasm and built my vocabulary (selling model script) to overcome objections from my customers. I quickly learned that "waving the Red, White and Blue" revs-up that emotional engine and helps builds relationships.

The selling model I started with had to be revised. Although my product was the same, my approach needed something more for this unfamiliar territory I had ventured into. It was the same type families, however, the relationship changed, because I was a "stranger" to these folks. The relationship dynamics morphed into simply one of being polite and superficial. Even though we lived within a mile of each other and I shared the same common language it was not enough to close the sale.

During that time I was learning a lot about building relationships. I realized I needed to build a trusting relationship with my customer before I began pushing their emotional buttons. I would begin with my name and identify myself as their neighbor from a few blocks away along with explaining my intentions. That is when new objections came along asking me why my parents allowed me to go door-to-door selling Christmas cards.

I started using the comments I heard my relatives use like, "Only in America can a neighborhood boy go door-to-door selling beautiful Christmas Cards and earn money". Sometimes this would work, but not enough for me to achieve my goal of a membership in the Album of the Month Club.

Just then the light bulb went off. I realized that reading an individual's body language and listening to their words were like "road signs". I could read their road signs. This was a way to size the customer up. This discovery helped me customize my approach.

If the potential customer smiled, that was a "road sign" that it was a warm welcome and I used the normal dialogue. If the customers "eye brows" went together with maybe a slight frown that was different "road sign" and I opened with "Only in America can these beautiful Christmas cards come right to your front door for you to pick one out" and "This will save you from having to wait for the stores to get their cards and you might chose the same ones your neighbor picks."

I even had a few prospects give me the road sign of a sharp curve. Their objection was they did not observe the Christmas holiday. My response, with a friendly smile was, "you do have friends that do celebrate Christmas and they would really love to receive one of these very beautiful cards from your family." Bingo, in the bank, sold! My response was natural and positive and perfectly fitting with the flow of our conversation.

Now I was having fun and closing deals. The music was playing in my head along with a big smile on my face. My father would tell me at the dinner table, "Son you're really onto something here, the salesman at our store need whatever it is you have." I was feeling invincible.

To my amazement my prospects started giving me legitimate objections. Crying out loud I would think. They would say, "I just spent all my money with the other salesman". No-way did I ever imagine that the vacuum guy or the brush guy could hurt my sales.

My business plan had to adjust again. Going forward I would look-out for those salesmen and go to the other block. Should another prospect tell me they just spent their money, my response was, "My family plans a budget too, let me give you my phone number for when you're ready." It worked like money in the bank.

It was not as much fun as in the beginning, until I completed another sale and then music would start playing in my head. The funny thought that came to my mind was "why are they including me with that adult?"

The only door-to-door guy I did not mind following was the "Charles Potato Chip" salesman because like my family they had that money planned to spend. So I would comment about that similarity we had in common. I found it helped the customer accept me quicker.

The comment would be something like, "Those chips are great, my mother is really happy with those chips because my whole family loves them" and then Bam! It happen the smile and warm greeting and then, BAM . . . Again a sale!

After the Christmas cards, which I sold for a few years, I started selling vegetable seeds, flower seeds. I would plant the same seeds in flower pots and pull them in my red wagon behind my bike to show what I was selling. WOW, my customers started asking for products that went with the seeds like planting soil or flower pots.

At the age of twelve I made the big times and started working at my father's paint store. They sold paint for aircraft, automotive, industrial and marine use. The name of the store was, B&L Paint Supply founded in 1953. That is when my door-to-door career had to stop. I was really surprised by how many customers called my home asking if I was still selling Christmas cards for a few years after that.

Working at the paint store was different in many ways. One thing for sure that was different was that the customers came to me or called the store. I thought this should make for a much easy sale. Another difference was that there really is no time to build relationships in the store like I had over the years with my neighbors.

Would I miss knocking on their front door? Sometimes while I was standing there at the front of their home, they felt compelled, even at our first meeting, to share a very happy experience they had receiving one of these type cards in the mail or just what a happy time of the year the holiday is.

Occasionally they would share something very sad about that time of year. Some of the stories centered on the Vietnam War because a lot of the young men that were drafted lived in the neighborhood, I learned.

Their parents would say, "we really don't feel like sending cards this year, sorry." I would answer them with something positive like, "your son would really think this one (pointing to a card) is very nice" and they would answer "yes" or "no, he would like this one I am sure of it" or "do you know him?" they would ask.

Most of them would begin to show an interest at that point. But really at that point making the sale was not as important as being a part of something good for them.

I would wait and listen to their story and really feel what they were explaining. I knew then that somehow this was part of the success even though I wanted to go to the next sale.

THE BEST RIGHT WORDS
AT THE RIGHT TIME

WHEN I STARTED working the sales counter at the paint store the Spanish speaking customers would be funneled towards me because Spanish is my first language. Growing up in a home where both Spanish and English were spoken turned out to be an advantage for me. It forced me to come up with words for things when there was no literal translation for those words (things). This also taught me that words and their meaning are a very big part of our life.

My mother explained to me that I spoke Spanish first and when I began going to school I learned English. Her English improved as my brother and I learned more English at school, but we still spoke Spanish on Saturdays when our relatives came over or until they began to perfect their English.

I realized early in my life that I had a knack for languages. I spent my school years focusing on the study of the power of words. Not only was the profound power of using an enriched vocabulary evident in school classes like history, geography and sociology, but it also played out every day in my own home between my family and my extended family who had emigrated from Cuba.

I have never spoken with an accent and this really was an asset when I began selling in Miami. However, my interest was piqued with the study of languages when I would witness individuals who had the abilities to listen and understand what is being said even though they did not understand the language that was being spoken to them.

When I would watch and listen to my family interacting and trying to translate words into each others' language sometime chaos would happen. Some words, like sandwich, do not translate into Spanish. When that happened you could see the frustration on my family members face and in their body language as they tried to find or create the word, sometimes it was funny and other times it was not so funny.

I remember the cook-out one Saturday afternoon when my father talked about his truck needing tires. You see in Spanish the word "tire" translates to "Llanta" however it depends on which Spanish speaking island you are from in the Caribbean because you might say "goma" which really means rubber but not to the person saying the word goma, they would use it for the word tire.

WOW! This started a war of words; comments laced with criticisms were flying all over the place both from the men and the women. That word goma from what they were saying is not Castilian Spanish for the word tire and my relatives would say that is the word a poor uneducated man would use for the word tire, I would hear. I quickly learned you are able to understand a lot about a person from the words they chose and their sentence structure.

As I started my first year at Cardinal Gibbons High School, some of my classes taught me how powerful and dominating some languages are over others. When one country conquered another country and then when they started trading one language had to be established as the standard.

This learning experience, and the scene that is etched in my memory from my family's heated discussions, ignited an immense spark in me that created a passion to study English and Spanish languages more intensely. This (that) experience lead me to writing out a personal goal of being more deliberately focused to choose the best words when communicating with others.

What helped create the confidence in me to be able to meet that personal goal was the weekly vocabulary test that was given to me through-out my Elementary and High School years. The Priest and Nuns that administered those test demonstrated a lot of interest in them.

After school I would work at the paint store. While I was working there opportunities to use my new vocabulary words were everywhere. But these older guys at the paint store, the average seller was twice my age or more, were not interested in my new "Best" choice words.

I noticed they would always use the same words they have used over the last several years in all their conversations. They had struggles with either trying to explain an issue or a challenge they were having with a co-worker or even with a customer on the phone. The unbelievable part is they were surprised when they did not achieve the results they wanted using their same old vocabulary.

It was like the employees and customers they were talking with were expecting those comments and had a personal "road map" pointing-out which objection to use to counter each point. This was very frustrating for me because there are better word choices that would streamline the communications and defuse the objection before it was addressed in their dialogue.

When I witnessed the communication struggle between one of our salesman and a customer at the sales counter it reminded me of the "war of words" between my family members. Part of the solution would be an agreed point or source of authority. For my family the agreed source of authority was my father. At the paint store the agreed source of authority would be the manufactures directions.

At the paint store sales counter I began to read the directions on the manufacture's labels so that I would be able to apply reasoning and facts in my sales script along with the manufactures' language.

The other sellers would ask me "why are you doing that?" I explained "to learn the manufactures' language" and they would laugh out loud. "So you are going to speak English, Spanish and sound like a paint label?" they said. I remember saying over and over again, "you do what works for you and I will do what makes money for me" that seemed to stop some of the laugher.

Only one of the six sellers asked me why was that going to make me money. I explained, "I will sound smart and this will build more confidence and trust in me with the customer," and "you watch they will start asking for me."

Within one week customers started requesting me to guide them to the proper product and procedure, if I did not know the answer I knew where to get it.

The next thing you know several of the other sellers were reading labels and directions at the counter. Surprisingly, complaints began to drop and moral at the sales counter went up. Just as importantly so did the sales.

After work one evening on the ride home my father explained that he and my mother had purchased a new set of encyclopedias for our family. He then told me of the expectations they had for us to use them.

Well one of the first subjects I turned to was languages and then to the diagram of the brain. In that chapter, along with related chapters, the facts that were being explained were very interesting. I learned that seventy percent of your brain is tied to visuals. So I am thinking it might be better for me to use descriptive words. I asked my teacher about this, she told me it is better when you use picture words in explanations.

My puzzled thoughts must have been written on my face and she said could read them. Here is an example she said, "It was so hot outside that I needed a whole ice cube tray of ice cubes to keep my soda cold." She then asked me if I "see" what she was talking about. I smiled and nodded.

After school it was time for work and time to apply my new knowledge. So I am thinking "picture words" for my sales approach. Just then a painter from a body shop came in and requested the best black lacquer paint because he had a show car to paint. I look him straight in the eye and said, "This particular black paint when you are finished with it will look as smooth as a wet ice-cube." That is the one for me! He said with a loud voice.

After he left with his paint the other sellers started laughing at me saying "where did that come from, as smooth as a wet ice cube". I told them there are more picture word sayings from where that came from. Some of them said, "It is a good thing you're the boss's son or we would kick you and your picture word sayings out of here."

Later that week the same painter came in asking for me. He said, "That paint finished sure look as slick as a wet ice cube", "but now I need the best clear-coat you have." I looked him in the eye and said, "With this clear coat you can read the time on your watch standing three feet away from the car."

He said, "I believe you, let me have enough to paint a Monte Carlo." The counter man standing next to me, said without thinking, "Hey Jerry don't you want to know how much it is?" and the customer answered, "No."

Double WOW! What just happened? The value that was perceived by that customer was so great that the price of the product did not matter. Yea, Baby, put it in the bank!

Later that night at the dinner table my dad commented to my mother about the difference it was making at work with the salesmen sounding more professional with their word choices. This was very nice and I felt empowered to go further because now this appeared to me as a science. If just changing your vocabulary will make that much of a positive increase in your earning abilities there has to be more, much more.

Would I be able to apply this technique with the Spanish speaking members of my family? What would that conversation sound like now? Would it still be a verbal "shoot-out" between family members? Some were insulted about the lack of "tact" that was used in arriving at the last conclusion. I vividly remember this because some of them did not visit us for months until they got over it or someone called to apologize.

It took a while and I was able to use this new technique of more picture words in my conversations with my Spanish speaking relatives with success.

That success fed my desire to learn more. When the new school year I had a plan that would start with the opening bell "like a starter pistol" at the track meet. My research was to begin with why the same words would generate different response in people. This really had me ready to race to where ever the answers are. This led me straight to psychology class and what I really was looking for were behavioral characteristics.

There was this question burning inside me. The question was; why would some customers just take my word for it regarding an answer to a question. Was it my title as the owner's son or that just being employed there with the proper shirt meant that you should know the answers? While others demanded more specifics answers and still others wanted step by step detail.

There must be indicators for which words certain people naturally use in their conversations and words they would gravitate too. Should there be these indicators then I would be able to predict the outcome of our conversation. I would know if they are just going to take my word for it or if they needed just a little detail or entire "step by step" explanation because I knew that words are like "road-signs".

I would study my relatives and my cousins with their word choices and the mannerisms they would employ when they would speak to others in and outside the family, along with asking them before and after their conversation what was your expectation and did you achieve your expectations.

My cousin would say, "Hey watch this I am going to ask Uncle Mike if he will buy us a pizza and he will just answer yes with no questions, he doesn't need all the details" and I would ask, "why not ask Grandpa". "Because the response will be totally different," my cousin would answer, "he will ask me a hundred questions, too much detail and I would died of starvation by the time we order the pizza and the pizza arrives here, that's why."

Now I thought we are "cooking with oil" there should be a process "a road map" that will give me the formula for a predictable outcome, based on behavioral characteristics with words. Where oh where do I find that goose that lays those golden eggs?

THE SCIENCE

THE SECOND YEAR at Cardinal Gibbons an opportunity to exercise and apply the power of words was made available through an elective class on the subject of Creative Writing. My thinking was this class would focus on best word choices. This would allow me to follow the path to where the goose that lays the golden eggs is. Little did I know at the time how wisely I chose.

Our wrestling coach was the teacher and it was a lot of fun. He explained to me that I need to follow my passion about the power of words because I have a gift of making the truth and facts exciting along with explaining things and telling stories. So I asked him for direction. He created the "next level" (on my lunch hour) for me to be able to take an upperclassman's elective class, which was psychology. The rules for engagement were to sit in class, listen and learn, and I was not allowed to comment or questions.

This class was really a challenge, not just for the material but in the upper-classman's class they are co-ed classes, which is different than our under-classman which are boys' only classes. The girls in this class sure were pretty and made those uniforms come alive.

The teacher of this class was the wife of one the football coaches and because I played most sports this seem to help her more easily accepted me. She gave me a book to use and I sat all the way in the back. She knew her material and taught the class with passion, which made it more fun.

And then one day this crazy question was directed to me, it was about taking a personality assessment along with an IQ test. I said what? This took place after school one day and I was amazed at the accuracy of the results of DISC personality assessment. The result of the IQ test was a score of 145. I wanted to know who invented this material and there had to be more.

The facts are that more than several hundred years before Christ, the Greek physician Hippocrates started this theory of DISC. His theory stated that there are four basic personalities or some would say temperaments. With that theory he began documenting and testing. Because he was a physician first, he started his research with the human body.

Hippocrates than connected the dots after selecting four body liquids that are predominated in the human body but are at different levels in certain temperaments. After selecting these four, the need to name them came into the theory. The names are Sanguine, Choleric, Melancholy and Phlegmatic.

The theory that different levels of certain body liquids would determine human personality traits has long been discarded but the four titles still exist and are used in psychology even today. What psychologist have been able to add to Hippocrates work are the definitions of "extrovert" and "introvert".

With this new knowledge, first my love for learning went to new heights and second the revelation that other people (who were geniuses) on the same planet from thousands of years ago also wanted to know the "code" for better communications. This started a desire in me to want to "look under every rock" read every book, attend any classes on the subject and I did.

Here is what I did. First, I reviewed my characteristics strengths and began to use them. Second, I learned the strengths of the other characteristics and began to "massage" those and record the results, first with my family and friends, then with my teachers. WOW! The results were very positive, productive and the dialogue was more fun. I started thinking more profits around the corner.

As my experience lead to better communication skills both personally and professionally, I needed more. This began an appetite for more reading, which un-covered a "treasure chest" of vocabulary words that are closely associated with the personality types, BINGO!

This was like "rubbing the lamp for the Jeanie" to be released and put to work. I started putting those words to work immediately in sales. This lead me to create a cataloged of words that I put into a play-book. So when I quickly identified which of the four personalities I had the pleasure of dealing with, I would refer to my "play book of words". This was a critical part of the formula to document. With that documentation there could be measurable results that may be predictable.

That is when the applications of the science of DISC really started putting money in the bank for me. Having achieved success both emotionally and monetarily it drove this desirer in me to record the successes and struggles.

This enabled me to continually review them so that I would know the material like the back of my hand. The value of this knowledge was enhanced because of my natural disposition of being charismatic and engaging.

This playbook had "trigger words" for each temperament that enabled me to have my point understood quicker with fewer words and to disarm the target's defenses. These words are like the "combination to a safe".

But then I wanted to know what else was working with the trigger words that made them work like "magic". What are the mechanics taking place in the mind and the physical parts of the brain? Which part of the brain is activated with these words and what type of chemical activities are firing-off and are they creating a "natural high" or are certain words creating some resistance.

Here is a snap-shot of what I learned and what the process looks likes.

Doctor Robert P. Lehr Jr., Ph.D. writes:
Professor Emeritus, Department of Anatomy, School of Medicine,
Southern Illinois University

CEREBRAL CORTEX <u>Frontal Lobe</u>: Most anterior, right under the forehead.

Functions:

- How we know what we are doing within our environment (*Consciousness*). How we initiate activity in response to our environment. Judgments we make about what occurs in our daily activities. Controls our emotional response. Controls our expressive language. Assigns meaning to the words we choose. Involves word associations.
- Memory for habits and motor activities.

To summarize in a "nutshell" the Cortex is: an "electronic fish net" which will "catch" what you are saying because you set-off the alarm with the words you used or did not use. This alarm is for the need for more in-depth analyst. This will "stop" the prospect from engaging in active listening and increase the opportunity of a "shoot-out". Or the "electronic fish net" permits your words to "swim through" and continue with the sale.

This is when you must "Deliberately be at your Best" with word choices. What I call "Trigger words" that are designed and tailored for each of the four communication types. With the balance of this book you will begin to learn the communication type of person you are speaking with and which trigger words to use.

Because where you want to go with the customer is the part of their brain which really is their "mind' which drives the imagination and emotions. This is where the opportunities for "possibilities" are able to grow coupled with strong emotions that will create a memory.

This is how the mind and brain work together: A guitar player selects the music he or she wants to perform, their mind actually selects the music and their brain plays it. The mind dictates and the brain executes it.

That is why you will be driving your vehicle and having a conversation on your cellular device and really not be thinking about driving because your mind is engage in the conversation (heavy lifting). Your brain is doing the task of driving the vehicle, you may even say to yourself, "how did I get here?" when you arrive at your final destination.

My research leads to the "mechanical working" of selected words within both the mind and brain. This really is my target audience because I want the customer's "engine" (mind) started and (emotions) running when it come time close the deal.

The best word choices work like a bag of microwaveable popcorn in the microwave (your customer's mind) and you push start. Quickly the corn starts popping (real meaningful productive dialogue) and there is no stopping it. Those are the same events that take place naturally in the mind when you use the best trigger words.

Physically what happens in the brain is the electron rich layer of the brain processes a word or something visual and your neurons begin the synapse and you cannot stop the thought process. I will give you an example.

If I were to ask most Americans to complete this statement: Red, White and… The majority of Americans would have thought Blue and they could not stop that thinking process. That process was a nanosecond and the same results with trigger works.

When you answer the question both in your mind and verbally, automatically the feelings of satisfaction that you answer the question correctly flood your mind. So are the memories associated with the thoughts of Red, White and Blue. This powerful mix of emotions you have associated with those words will drive your decision making.

Our experiences are stored away in our memory with words, emotions, sounds, smells and visuals. As you will learn each of the four character traits with DISC are attracted with different trigger words to activate those emotional responses.

What does it look like physically? The next few paragraphs outlines are a brief description.

Information is transferred from short-term memory (also known as working memory) to long-term memory through the hippocampus, so named because its shape resembles the curved tail of a seahorse (hippocampus in Greek). The hippocampus is a very old part of the cortex and is located in the inner fold of the temporal lobe.

All of the pieces of information decoded in the various sensory areas of the cortex converge in the hippocampus, which then sends them back where they came from. The hippocampus is a bit like a sorting centre where these new sensations are compared with previously recorded ones. The hippocampus also creates associations among an object's various properties.

When we remember new facts by repeating them or *by employing various mnemonic devices*, we are actually passing them through the hippocampus several times. The hippocampus keeps strengthening the associations among these new elements until, after a while, it no longer needs to do so. The cortex will have learned to associate these various properties itself to reconstruct what we call a memory.

the**brain**.mcgill.ca/flash/d/d_07/d . . . /d_07_cr_tra.html

The next event that takes place, if you really did "crack the code" with the trigger words you used in the sales cycle, is a movie playing in your prospects mind. This movie was created by their imagination and memory. Your prospect or customer is "seeing" the product or solution you are selling, actually working in this movie playing in their mind. "Bam!" You did it! Enjoy the movie and keep the popcorn hot!

With the majority of people having experienced day dreaming they will be able to accept this explanation. Our minds will tap into this power instantly to create a brief visual of what we are attempting to understand.

What that looks like physically is this:

At the Sleep Neuroimaging Research Program at the University of Pittsburgh Medical Center, researcher Eric Nofzinger, MD, delves into the brains of sleeping subjects using PET scans normally employed to detect cancer and other diseases. By injecting subjects with mildly radioactive glucose, he's traced the source of dreams to the limbic system, a primitive part of the brain that controls emotions. During dreaming, the limbic system explodes like fireworks with neural activity, suffusing our dreams with drama.

That's why so many dreams are emotional events," says Nofzinger, "where we're running from danger or facing an anxious situation. The part of the brain that controls dreams also orchestrates our instincts, drives, sexual behavior and fight-or-flight response." Meanwhile, the frontal lobes of the brain that govern logic disengage, explaining why dreams are often bizarre combinations of events and people.

From *Reader's Digest–February 2006*

Because all of this is happening at once with you and your customer, or prospect, there is a great opportunity for your communication and your customer's communication to have created two different movies (products or solutions) playing in each other's mind.

I have seen and heard this happen many times both with face to face meetings as well as on the phone sales. The first real indicator this has happen is when your customer will make the statement, "I thought you said . . ." or "I thought you meant this . . ." In reality you probability did say what is correct for you to tell the customer but the "movie" playing in their mind "lead" them to understand differently.

Now, that is no excuse for a lying salesman or a lying customer, which there are both. But for the honest sales person with integrity and ethical standards the above situation is a reality.

I have worked with both types of sales professionals. The honest sales person may make a statement that was dictated by the company they were representing and later learn that the particular statement was not completely accurate or not accurate at all. Should that occur the sales person with integrity will give a brief explanation. Using the trigger words for the type of communicator they are will enable their customer to better understand the explanation.

So how did that situation happen? Two or more people engaging in a meaningful, productive conversation see two different products or solutions when you both are discussing the same product and solution? Let's take a quick look and then we will outline the four types of communication types and the trigger words.

What happened is the electronic fish net was disengaged and the creative thinking process was in full swing which opened the door to a multiple of possibilities of usage with your product and solutions.

Depending on each individuals' "natural wiring" for communication will be the deciding factor whether only the facts will be addressed and heard or whether the presenter or customer are not interested in the facts but just the big picture along with a brief timeline of when it can be accomplished.

In the computer, which is your brain, there are several dynamic systems working at once, your body, mind, spirit and emotions are always interacting. There is a measuring of the dynamics of your vocabulary, body language, eye contact and pictures you are creating in the presentation.

When you are selling over the phone your vocabulary has to be unlimited and powerful because you are working without the benefit of eye contact and without the ability of reading their body language. The need is still there to address all the dynamic systems working in your customers' mind and brain.

The four characteristics we are going to work with are:

The Take Charge Choleric, Natural born leader.
The Always Fun Sanguine, Perfect motivator.
The Easy Going Phlegmatic Always keeps their cool.
The Melancholy, Critical Thinker.

Most individuals have a little blend of all the above characteristics. There typically is one temperament that truly dominates and that would be the default behavior. You will be able to quickly identify their communication strength(s) after completing this book.

We want to be selective with our words and design our communications to excel with business. Just like a tailor or a seamstress understands that not all men's' suites or women's suites on the rack perfectly fit everyone, they are a good start but for the perfect finish there must be some selective adjustments.

Here are the tools.

CHOLERIC

THE TAKE CHARGE Choleric is the letter "D" for Direct on the DISC scale.

These individuals' natural strengths are: Most always being Practical and decision making is easy for themselves as well as making decisions for other people you may conclude they are decisive and opinionated. The "D" is quick to recognize opportunities and equally as bright in understanding the best avenues to apply them.

The "D" has relentless determination and will succeed not because of a better plan but because the "D" is always moving forward, even at the cost of others opinions or feelings. The results are paramount not the details or obstacles that may be in the way.

How do I recognize a high "D" communicator?

Here are some of the signs:

Their speech patterns are Clear, Confident and Direct. I like to say, there is "steel in their voice".

Clothing: They are most always wearing the appropriate apparel for the occasion and it will most always be nicely pressed and color coordinated.
Conversation style: Fast, direct and may feel like they are abrupt. The "D" enjoys being a little argumentative and impatient.

Emotional feedback: Limited at best, independent, may sound like anger at times.

Face to Face meeting: Direct eye contact is best and a firm, even a strong handshake sends the best message. Allow for reasonable space between you and the "D" but lean into or towards that individual when communicating. You must be very consciences of your hand and body movements, too many and you are gone. Should you be walking to their office or somewhere with them, the "D" likes to walk fast.

How do I work with this person's natural strengths?

1. Be direct in your conversation, have your bullet points prepared and use them, this person is a very practical, keen "thinking" machine, prefers to make an instant decision that are typically very sound.
2. You have to listen quickly, because they speak to "bullet points" and listen for "bullet points" only and your bullet points are your key points.
3. Very little if any small talk and they may want to "Lock Horns" with you (argumentative) and this is normal behavior for a "D" and should there be a "locking of the horns" regarding your product or solution, as long as it is not a buying objection (may be a procedural objection), this would be considered a "green light" towards closing the deal.
4. You do not have to talk as fast as they do, this is not a competition. But talking fast between two "D's" is normal and acceptable to a degree. Because you want to "lead" the customer and to accomplish that you need to manage the conversation. Or the end result will be a conversation between two loud, confident, opinionated "D's" that have express their opinions and no sale.
5. Do not "tell them" what they must do, "D's" prefer to discover and analyze the product or solution with little detail along the way and you need a clear pronounced end result. This person prefers a conversation that is very much a two-way street. You would make your point, pause for few seconds and then seek (read their body language, fascicule gestures) their input.
6. Permit alternatives or some flexibilities, they are "in-charge" they need to make the decision. They need to win.
7. Remember the Win-Win. Close the deal, money in the bank.

Trigger words and phrases: listed below are the "bags of microwaveable popcorn".

New Improved	Few restrictions	Streamline
Procedure	Few details	Automatic
Best Product	No task is too big	No wasted time
Now available now	You WIN	Results, Results, Results
Change	Challenge	Leader

The following example has the Trigger words underlined for you. This is a template that you would use with a "D" type communicating prospect.

I always dress for success with coordinated dry-cleaned slacks, shirt and especially for the "D" customer's because the "mind" of a "D" is going to acknowledge in a positive manner my appearance and the "electronic fish net" will begin to lower its defense and allow the trigger words to get through.

This is a real-life example; I was a sub-contractor sales representative for a software company that produced "management software" for any automotive repair collision center industry.

My first tier of targets were the Mercedes Benz automotive repair collision centers because typically their customer base are very demanding for results and this software does everything (about a hundred different functions to manage those demands) for this type of facility. There for it was a perfect fit. They would easily recognize the value of those results the software produced.

I was on a follow-up/cold call because the manager and I had met briefly at a local industry meeting but did not really schedule a meeting in the future; he just invited me to stop by his facility anytime I was in the area. In this automotive industry I was very well known and liked as well as respected (15 plus years) for computer software sales designed for this trade.

During this brief encounter I addressed the issue of offering a solution with measurable results for streamlining processes for his business that required little detail from the person entering the data. I used those trigger words for a "D" because of the indicators Ryan was giving with his dress, fast pace walk and his strong voice.

Now, this is what happened: I took the opportunity to be in his business area. I walked into the reception area and asked the receptionist if I might speak with Ryan the facilities' manager. She asked if he was expecting me. I answeedr "no" but I have the <u>step by step</u> answers to all his problems and handed her my card and ask her to call him, please. I used the trigger words for an "S" type communicator because of the indicators she gave me.

She smiled back and said, "Ok," When Ryan was on the phone with her, she explained that I had all the steps that would answer all of his problems" and then she said, "I don't know which problems but he has the steps and a nice briefcase with him." She very politely looked at me and explained that he would be here in a minute.

Ryan walked with a <u>fast pace</u> into the reception area and I greet him with a <u>hardy handshake</u> and, looking <u>directly</u> in his <u>eyes,</u> re-introduce myself referencing the industry meeting and his invitation for me to stop by.

He smiled and said, "Oh yes, I remember now". His next question was <u>direct</u> and he asked how long is this going to take? I answer that is <u>your decision</u> either fifteen minutes or thirty minutes.

Ryan's <u>third decision</u> in just several minutes was that fifteen minutes are going to be enough for him to understand what I am offering. We walked back in a<u> hurried</u> fashion and I really had to work at walking that fast.

When we arrived at his office there were the piles of folders and papers lying around in no particular order on his desk confirmed his "D" communicator style because of. We sat down and he said, "Tell me what this is all about."

I said, "Our understandings about your software needs are: You need it <u>right</u> <u>now</u> the <u>best product</u> with <u>few restrictions</u> to <u>streamline</u> communication to every department with a <u>few details</u> about the repair that is <u>automatically</u> generated and <u>no wasted time</u> and it <u>will produce</u> positive bottom-line <u>results</u> <u>immediately</u> with <u>no task to big</u>, so <u>you win</u> the <u>challenge</u>".

Ryan, with this happy look, asked "what is the drawback?" I answered, <u>"change."</u>

He then said, "How did you know this is exactly what I have been thinking?" and "No one has this product." BINGO! The next question from him was, "Where is this and when can I see it?"

I opened my briefcase and handed him a PowerPoint presentation on a CD and answer, "Ryan it is all here for <u>you</u> to <u>decide</u> when to review it and I will write down the facilities that are using the product now" and "Because my fifteen minutes is almost done, I will respect our agreement regarding time and follow-up with you . . . what date is good for you?"

He then decided to ask, "Well how much is this software?"

I said, "What does it matter? It does everything and it is <u>available now!</u>"

He continued, "How much?"

And I said, "How much do you think?"

Ryan's face was not looking very happy right then, he said, "I don't know." I answered him quickly, you are an intelligent man you have a very good idea, just use your imagination, picture all the tasks this will complete and the results it will achieve. I paused for a minute and asked "can you picture this?" . . . and he said, "yes I can."

COME ON SOMEBODY! Is what I thought.

He guessed around eighty thousand dollars. If Ryan were to purchase all the modules of the software it would be twenty-five thousand plus a monthly support fee of two hundred dollars, which at that time was the standard fee for support.

"I like your guess and if you had the time to make the decision while I am here because you would be the first Mercedes facility in Miami with this entire package, including several of the hand-held devices, the price is twenty five thousand."

He said, "Ok," which to me meant the deal is not closing today. "How about the price tomorrow?" he asked.

I replied, "I don't know because I am scheduled for the balance of this week to be in another area and I only need a five thousand dollar check to lock this in while I am here and your solution is on its way with a thirty-day money-back return, it is clearly only your decision to call the Comptroller and request a check."

Ryan looked me straight in the eyes and said, "I was not expecting to write you a check today."

My response was honest, "I was deliberately planning that when all the tools in this program are working for you, you will be the leader in our industry because your management skills will be enhance and the battle of achieving greater results will be in your favor. With all that, I thought you would decide to permit me to become a productive member of your team."

"Let's get your check then," he said. FOR CRYING OUT LOUD, MONEY IN THE BANK!

THE SANGUINE

THE ALWAYS FUN Sanguine, Perfect motivator is the letter "I" for Interesting on the DISC scale.

These individuals' natural strengths are:

Mostly happy, and enthusiastic, loves to have fun and interact. Always quick with a story that when they tell it, the "I" is so compelling you think they are reliving the actual event again. The Sanguine is usually, very witty and a gifted speaker, and typically loud. Very optimistic and is everyone's friend. The biggest and warmest smile is normal for the "I".

The "I" believes they are the life of the party and they will motivate everyone to be involved and have a good time. When you see an "I" walking down the street they automatically have to say, "hi" to everyone that crosses their path.

The "I" has relentless desire to have recognition (which can be as simple as a thank you) and will focus on the future. Details and facts may get in the way of having fun. This person is attracted to risk and they flow with either the success or the failure.

The journey and the people involved with the journey are most important. When an "I" says, "I feel your joy or your sorrow" they really, really do genuinely mean that.

How do I recognize a high "I" communicator?

Here are some of the signs:

Their speech pattern is: High energy with high and low modulation, Enthusiastic, Fast, Personal and Witty.

Clothing: Casual Sloppy

Conversation style: Engaging and very personable

Emotional feedback: Excitable with noticeable "highs" and "lows"

Face to Face meeting: Likes the "touchy feely", handshakes (not to strong, unlike the "D") and or hugs. It is good to be physically close (within reason about two feet away) but not as far away like a "D" (three feet or more). You need to be relaxed, friendly eye contact, some humor (wit) with physical gestures that are expressive.

Sanguine

How do I work with this person's natural strengths?

1. Your conversation either in person or over the phone must be stimulating; they prefer the dialogue to be a little impulsive along with a little details or facts.
2. You need to allow them to speak; along with you being engaging, that means you will need to interrupt and follow-up or re-follow-up on your point.
3. Your conversation needs to have a little humor and you need to provide recognition; the "I" graves entertainment along with you verbally acknowledging their "skills" to motivate people to "Make it Happen".
4. You do not have to talk as fast as they do, this is not a competition. You need to be a little slower than they are. But never ever belittle them.
5. Do have brief testimonies of other customers, in your description of your products and services "high light" the opportunity and risks.
6. Briefly list the chain of events that will take place without great detail, Paper-work to a Sanguine is like kryptonite for Superman
7. Remember it is normal for this individual to over-commit, to avoid a "shoot-out" ask who are the other members, "not the decision makers because you should already know who the decision maker is or are", who will be involved and who will be carrying-out what needs to be done. Because it is a real challenge for an "I" do get it done, it is easier for them to come-up with the idea and delegate the details. The more "key" people they are able to have involved the better.

Trigger words and phrases: listed below are the "bags of microwaveable popcorn".

Fun	Futuristic	Few restrictions
Exciting	Your ideas are great	Few details
Everyone will be involved	Risk	Opportunities
Everyone will be thanking you	I feel really good	Feel the love

The following example has the *Trigger* words underlined for you. This is a template that you would use with an "I" type prospect or customer in communicating.

Always dress for success with coordinated dry cleaned slacks and shirt, all your customers expect a professional to look and sound professional. Your attire and vocabulary typically should be one grade above your prospect or customer.

This is a real-life example; I was a sales representative at the time for a National Paint Manufacture and the person I was meeting was in the business of painting large commercial jets.

As I watched Juan approach me to welcome me, I quickly noticed his big smile and enthusiastic loud hello and in this situation I somewhat mirrored his greeting and that was recorded, recognized by his "electronic fish net" which began to lower its defense and allow the trigger words to get through.

Juan and I have never met but our companies had been doing business for a while and his office phoned our office, which sent me there. As we walked to his office there was some conversation which was initiated by Juan. He asked in one sentence two questions quickly, "How was the traffic? "Did you find us easily?"

My answer was in an evenly paced manner, "The journey was fun and your parking is full, how many people work here?"

"Oh there are a lot of people. We do everything for the planes," Juan said with a smile.

"That sounds like a lot of fun and exciting, you must have a lot of very good ideas about what can be done looking into the future of this business, and I would love to hear them."

"Well they are a little risky," he said without taking a breath. "Our company is where it is today because of some good risk and some risk we had to work-through."

Once we arrived at his office, it was easy to notice the very bright and lively colors along with the action pictures with the motivational posters with team building focus.

WOW! This is like being in a motivational center or a sports bar, everybody must want to have their meeting in here or just hang out, with a big smile, I complement him on how "lively" his office looks and asked him to tell me about some of the plaques he had earned that were on the wall after about ten minutes we sat down at his desk.

Juan commented on how happy he and his department were that this appointment was easy to make, "just one call". Our other clients had told us how important that was, so we took the opportunity to make that a priority and the risk paid off.

I then asked him to explain all his ideas that would concern our two companies and the he felt should be addressed now and three to five years from now along with offering him the opportunity to invite colleagues from other departments in to share their ideas and to please feel free to explain that you arranged for my company to have me here. BAM!

He gave me about a dozen very good ideas and invited several other department heads into the meeting, which I schedule follow-up appointments for the next several days as not to "bore" Juan.

My answer to his ideas and needs was, "Juan these ideas are great, exciting, fun and futuristic for your company. A lot of people will be involved, everyone will be thanking you. There are some risks and like you, I see them as opportunities. You should feel really pretty good because there are few restrictions and to show you some love, my company will take care of "all the details."

Juan said, "Where do I sign?" And my response was, "after the first month, should your team spend five thousand dollars, with less than five percent credit will have a party here for lunch under your directions." He said, "Let's do it, do it, do it!"

HOT COFFEE! Money in the bank!

PHLEGMATIC

T HE EASY GOING Phlegmatic is the letter "S" for Sensitive on the DISC scale.

These individuals' natural strengths are: Being an excellent listener. Attracted to facts and has a passion to serve. The Phlegmatic is predicatively calm and orderly or methodical along with an "eagle eye" for detail. They do enjoy friendship and possess a naturally dry sense of humor.

The "S" desires a peaceful existence and by many considered a natural peace-maker. You will often find that the "S" enjoys people watching along with a capability of having a "knack" (their dry humor) for "needling" people. You are able to count-on-them being loyal, agreeable and supportive. You must remember to show your appreciation either verbally or a written note, email or an award.

How do I recognize a high "S" communicator?

Here are some of the signs:

Their speech pattern is, Soft, Steady, Low volume, uses "warm" words.
Clothing: They are most always wearing business casual.
Conversation style: The Best regarding a real "two-way" flow and personable, however indirect with their own opinions, very much like a diplomat.
Emotional fee-back: Warm and friendly, you can expect a call to action but the "S" is a real spectator and is reluctant to any activity aside from their daily routine.

Face to Face meeting: You need friendly eye contact, polite hand shake and small physical gestures with your hands and body. You need to be prepared to walk slowly and a little small talk too.

Phlegmatic

How do I work with this person's natural strengths?

1. Your conversation in person or over the phone must be pleasant; they prefer the dialogue to be "peppered" with facts.
2. You need to wait for a response; along with you being friendly and engaging, do not interrupt them.
3. Your conversation needs to address and discuss their feelings; the "S" builds relationships and a "corner stone" of that process is to discuss both your feelings in the beginning, middle and throughout the entire process.

You do not have to talk as slow as they do, be yourself. A clear indicator that you are talking too fast is when you find yourself repeating a lot of what you just said. So plan your dialogue and chose your words.

Do have brief testimonies of other customers, in your description of your products and services "high light" what their feelings were through-out the entire process including you or your companies follow-up.

Briefly list the chain-of-events that will take place without great detail, the "S" is focus on the present, outline the chain of events but not too far into the future.

For the high "S" they are reluctant to initiate change, You need to provide assurance about going forward and address the input of others that will build a collective opinion that this is next step in being more productive and profitable with very little if any confrontation from any and all parties involved.

Trigger words and phrases: listed below are the "bags of microwaveable popcorn".

Step by Step	Present	Relationships
Guarantee	Help me out	Consensus
Harmony	Service	Appreciation
Promise	Think about it	Here are the facts

The following example has the Trigger words underlined for you. This is a template that you would use with an "S" type prospect or customer in communicating.

In this real life example, I was working for a Tax Attorney Strategist and the lion-share of our sales were over the phone. There was a list that was generated from a website that offered a free audio CD from this attorney and on the web-site you could elect to have someone follow-up with a call.

Here is what happens: When I checked the area code for the phone number I was calling, I could see that it was from the Mid-west (which usually dictates an "S" type communicator) and the name is Mr. Hamilton. I dial the number and the prospect answered the phone on the first attempt.

With a very polite hello (low key) from the prospect, I responded, "<u>Hello</u> (low key) this is LW with . . . Mr. Hamilton and this is your <u>follow-up</u> call which is a free <u>service</u> to you," and I waited an "un-convertible" whole minute for a response which was, "Oh, yes, this is from the CD."

I would like to <u>share</u> with you the <u>facts</u> addressed on the CD and <u>permit</u> me to answer any <u>questions</u> you or <u>any member</u> of your <u>office</u> may have. Again I waited an un-convertible whole minute and the response was, "I would <u>like</u> <u>more</u> of the <u>facts</u>," and how does this all work and please call me Jack. Before I answered him I waited almost a whole minute.

Very good Jack, let's take this <u>step-by-step </u>because we do <u>appreciate</u> your time. The first import <u>fact</u> is your first <u>step</u> in the <u>right direction </u>is ordering and listening to the CD. What <u>questions</u> to you have about the important information on this CD Jack?

After a few seconds his response was, "Do I tell my CPA that <u>they need</u> to <u>be a part</u> of this?"

My answer, "That is an <u>excellent</u> question, yes; because he or she is a <u>member of your team</u> and the <u>fact</u> is this question does come-up because of that <u>we</u> have a program <u>available for both</u> you and your CPA because it is sometimes a <u>precondition for improvement</u> with the process of filing your tax report." Next question, "How does that work?"

"Another <u>excellent question, however,</u> before I answer that, <u>my</u> I ask <u>you a</u> <u>question Jack?</u>"

"Yes, sure what is your question Larry?"

My questions are: "Please <u>explain</u> to me <u>everything you do</u> and <u>your</u> <u>goals</u> along with how <u>our team</u> of <u>professionals</u> along with <u>our guaranties and</u> <u>assurances,</u> fit into your <u>business plan</u> and <u>goals</u>?"

Jack said, "I am <u>responsible</u> for a Hedge-fund and <u>we</u> are investing in property in Cape Coral Florida, <u>we</u> need to legally reduce are tax liabilities and this <u>sounds</u> like maybe you can <u>help</u> me but <u>I don't</u> pretend to think I can <u>tell</u> my CPA something he already knows."

"The leader of a Hedge-fund is a tremendous <u>service</u> which is <u>greatly</u> <u>appreciated,</u>" was my timely response and Jack with a quicker response added,

"I really did not want this role but my friends (investors) all fifteen of them insisted that I do it."

"You have addressed several Key Performance Points which really are Key facts that we build are business and relationships around, one we do reduce your tax liabilities legally, two it does sound great and the thousands of individuals and business we have help know and understand it just doesn't sound great, it is great and three we don't pretend to tell CPA's their job either."

Mr. Hamilton was my first Platinum customer. Put the money in the bank, Baby!

THE MELANCHOLY, CRITICAL THINKER

T HE MELANCHOLY CRITICAL Thinker is the letter "C" for Careful on the DISC scale.

These individuals' natural strengths are:

Most always very well organized and dressed appropriately. Always appear to be under control and never lack for self-disciplined. The "C" is committed to a standard of excellence along with being orderly and thorough.

The "C" has a very sensitive nature and because of their "natural" attentiveness to detail they are able to review all the positives and all the negatives of most every issue, which is one of the reasons they are genius-prone.

The "C" is genuinely concerned about the effects of change and is emotionally responsive but will not verbalize them quickly however the "C" will experience deep reflective thinking with their emotions assisting in the process.

For the "C" making friends are with caution, they are faithful and will dedicate themselves completely to a purpose. They will be moved to tears when showing compassion.

How do I recognize a high "C" communicator?

Here are some of the signs:

Their speech pattern is: Slow-methodical
Clothing: Business Appropriate
Conversation style: Controlled, Direct, Thoughtful, not to high not to low
Emotional fee-back: Sensitive, careful
Face to Face meeting: Keep your distance, firm posture, direct eye contact and
  absolutely no gestures.

Melancholy

How do I work with this person's natural strengths?

1. Your conversation either in person or over the phone must be stimulating,
    they are a very good listener and especially in relations to task details.
2. You need to allow them to be right, along with supporting their thoughts.
3. Your conversation needs to be precise, logical and loaded with data, the
    "C" needs proof and evidence.
4. You do not have to talk as slow as they do, this person typically takes
    time to gather facts before making decisions, is deliberately thorough and
    competent.
5. Do have brief testimonies of other customers, with the focus on the past
    and the detail (which may seem painful for you but is important for the
    "C") of the progress and success now.
6. List the chain-of-events that will take place with great detail, this person
    has a Herculean appetite for charts, graphs, lists and figures.
7. The "C" avoids tension but is persistent and thorough, because they are
    persistent they will appreciate that character trait in you and you must
    outline how you are going to follow through on your promises along with
    providing evidence.
8. Should you be meeting the "C" in person be prepared to walk fast and your
    conversation needs to be direct and attentive to detail, you need to manage
    the time because the "C" will get "caught-up" in the details and not be
    concerned with the time.

Trigger words and phrases: listed below are the "bags of microwaveable popcorn".

Here are the facts	No risk	Past history
Data	Warrantee	Proven
Analysis	Documented	Accuracy
Volumes of data	Deliberate	Perfectionist

The following example has the Trigger words underlined for you. This is a template that you would use with a "C" type prospect or customer in communicating.

Here is the scenario. My friend is selling software to the mechanical industry. This software which could be installed on a handheld personal devise and will enable the master mechanic to either speak into or type onto the devise (right at the vehicle or on their desk) what appears to be the problem with the engine and the software will give suggestions as to what maybe the problem along with solutions.

The typical target mechanical shop for this product is a high-end repair facility, Ferraris, Aston Martins, Bentley's, Mercedes and more.

The mechanical shop is in Miami and I made certain that Stuart had several graphs in color along with charts. As we met (schedule appointment) with Mr. Hess, there was no handshake just a polite "How do you do" and a brisk walk back to his office.

As we approached his office, I made mention the customer's path to the office entrance how the design has reduced or just about eliminated the customer's ability to "walk-into" danger. Mr. Hess commented that "not everyone" takes notice of the care we designed to avoid trouble.

As the sales' call progresses I took the lead with, "Mr. Hess we want to be direct and precise with the volumes of data we have along with our printed critical analysis that is sensitive to day to day task and detail that is unique to your industry and to the high standard you have established for your business."

"Well let me see all of it!" was his response.

I said, "Here are the first four books for you with charts and graphs along with a few lists. Please be thorough with your attention to detail because we want to be right by your standards and with the historical data here, we hope you agree that we have measured the positives and negatives which enables us to provide the evidence for a increase in your profitability along with a proven streamlining of the process for the repair which will reduce any effect of change, we guarantee."

"WOW, how did you memorize all that? Who is this guy I don't know if I want to sign now or buy him a drink!"

"Mr. Hess, in this report we have bullet points that list the facts along with the documentation of our successes with a summary of each along with phone numbers for you to contact and our no-risk guarantees," is my follow-up.

"Well first I have to really think about this," with a small smile from Mr. Hess. "Please share your thoughts with us," Stuart fired-off.

"We are in no rush," I remember, Mr. Hess just looking at the written mechanical manuals in his office, like he was not listening, as I spoke those words opening.

That sales call was three hours long and it was like wrestling with an eight-legged octopus because he was romanticizing using his books (holding the books and knowing exactly what page a particular repair could be found along with the weight, smell, leather cover, the excitement of receiving the new books every year)and the whole slow process.

We wanted to wrap duct tape around our heads to keep them from exploding. This guy had the first wrench he received forty years ago. And that was our ticket into this world of change he was very, very slow to embrace.

He bought and paid for a package worth forty thousand dollars. His testimony helped closed five more deals.

Hot Coffee! C'MON SOMEBODY! MONEY IN THE BANK!

WHAT IS YOUR NATURAL COMMUNICATION TYPE?

S ELECT AND CIRCLE your answers to the questions below. Do not select answers you think others want you to select.

1) Which word appeals to you most:	1. Now 2. Fun 3. Step by Step 4. Details
2) It is normal for me to be:	1. Forceful 2. Expressive 3. Restrained 4. Careful
3) I like to be:	1. Pioneering 2. Exciting 3. Satisfied 4. Correct

4) It is good to be:	1. Bold 2. Animated 3. Willing 4. Precise
5) There are times when I am:	1. Argumentative 2. Unpredictable 3. Indecisive 4. Doubting
6) It is important to be:	1. Daring 2. Outgoing 3. Patient 4. Respectful
7) I am:	1. Self-reliant 2. Persuasive 3. Gentle 4. Logical
8) It is easy for me to be:	1. Decisive 2. Life of the party 3. Even-tempered 4. Cautious
9) It is easy for me to be:	1. Assertive 2. Popular 3. Generous 4. Perfectionist
10) I am:	1. Strong-willed 2. Playful 3. Friendly 4. Observant

Let's score your answers

Answer sheet:				
Place a check mark under the number you circled in each row.				
Question Number	One/**D**	Two/**I**	Three/**S**	Four/**C**
One				
Two				
Three				
Four				
Five				
Six				
Seven				
Eight				
Nine				
Ten				
Enter the number of checks plus the letter				
Enter letters from highest to lowest				

The score above reflects from the highest score which is your natural communication strength to the lowest which you appreciate but is not your dominate trait.

It is possible to have a tie and it is possible to have your scores within one or two points of each other.

What do the four different types look like going out to Starbucks?

Well let's start with the letter "D". Let's say the "D" is driving, so be certain to buckle up your safety belts.

The "D" will race to the store location in their natural state of being a "D". Once they have arrived the "D" prefers the drive-thru window. But if the "D" has to enter the store, walking at a fast pace to enter the store and should there be more than several people in line it is possible for the "D" to leave and if not the "D" will watch like a hawk how productive everyone who is working there is or is not.

It is likely the "D" may speak out loud regarding the need for their order to be handled quickly along with making faces and or sounds. Once the "D" has received their order it is a quick exit and it will not be long until they have enjoyed their purchase quickly.

Now the "I" is going to have a party on the journey to Starbucks. The "I " will inform everyone that is possible they are going to Starbucks, not to necessarily to take an order and bring something back but if you want to join in the journey the more the merrier and a greater recipe for drama.

Along the way the "I" may change the radio station several times along singing-out-loud with each song and or there maybe multiple subjects if there is a conversation taking place.

Once arriving at the location the "I" should there be an audience will solicited opinions whether or not to enter the store or the drive-thru and if someone should say, "Oh look so-and-so car is here," the "I" will want to go into the store or just for the adventure to see who and what is happening in the store.

Once in the store the "I" will naturally comment and engage everyone possible in a very positive atmosphere how wonderful it is to be there and everybody and everything is great including the music.

The "I" will say hello and goodbye to almost everyone on their exit. When the "I" has arrived at their next destination (event) everyone will hear a great story about their experience earlier in the day.

The "S" prepares to leave and may or may not ask a friend if they would to go and if they would want anything. The "S" unlike the "D" or "I" will obey the speed limit and if there are a few traffic lights, well the lights are part of the process. The radio will be on a soft jazz or a music station with some polite small talk.

The "S" really does not like to be in a rush, so the drive-thru is not a big temptation and it is not as personable. The "S" will hold the door open for others to enter or exit and will expect that individual to say "Thank you". Once inside if there are several people in-line the "S" figures this must be a consensus of how it is done.

The "S" will say hello if someone greets them first. What is important for the "S" is to be pleasant, warm and friendly. Oh let's not forget the "dry sense" of humor.

Once the "S" arrives at their next destination, life continues without a skipping a beat.

The "C" will consider the pros and cons of several possible routs before choosing one. The time of day, the weather and exactly how much time the travel will take to arrive there along with the time at that location it typically takes for the processing of an order and the time to travel to their next destination along with how much time they have to enjoy their purchase.

Should the radio be on, because it may not if there is a lot of "thinking" taking place for the "C", it will be on a station with data or information being address or talk about, typically.

Once at the location the "C" considers the best parking spot and again several thoughts are being consider, which will include any danger or obstacles that could come into play along with the exit strategy.

Upon leaving the vehicle should the drive-thru not be a positive option, the "C" will walk briskly but not a "fast" as a "D" into the store. If there are several people in front of the "C", they will calculate how much time it should take to process each person's order which will cause them to either smile because their earlier calculation is accurate or they may not smile because they have to re-calculate.

While waiting in line they will review each step in the process and formulate an improved procedure and wonder why no-one from the company has figured it out. The "C" will engage in polite conversation if there is some information or data being shared if not a smile or a nod of the head will work for the "C".

How do you conduct yourself now?

You need to apply this science now and there are several steps to "coach" you through. We want to build "muscle memory" in your brain, so when your mind recognizes the "clues" or "behavioral traits", BAM, you have deliberately selected the best words to communicate.

The following pages are tests for you to take to apply your skills. Read the scenario and answer what type of communicator is the customer. In the "Why" section of the answer, you will need to answer what was the "clue" or indicator for your decision.

Test number one.

You are a phone solicitor and your prospect or customer is on the phone. You say, "Good morning, this is Ethan, I am calling today for your warranty on your . . . Your prospect or customer response is: "Good morning" with enthusiasm.

What type of communicator is this customer ____
Why _____

Test number two.

You are a pharmaceutical representative and you have several medical doctors schedule for today's sales and follow-up calls.

What type of communicator is this customer typically ____
Why _____

Test number three.

You are a customer service representative handling phone calls from customers with issues with your companies' credit card machines. You have a customer on the phone who is the manager at a restaurant and his first few comments to you are said very fast and with a strong tone, "I need this now!" "You need to fix this now!"

What type of communicator is this customer ____
Why _____

Test number four.

You are a multi-line insurance sales person. Your customer is sitting in your office dressed casual, but not too casual. They are always very pleasant to deal with and a very good listener. However, this customer always needs a little more assurance to make a change.

What type of communicator is this customer ____
Why _____

Test number five.

You are a financial advisor. Your customer of several years has a million dollars invested with your company. Currently, this customer wants more detail and data about a certain investment. There is no more information available. But, you have noticed that this customer has a habit of overstating the facts and this is troubling because normally this customer is very detailed and very organized.

What type of communicator is this customer ____
Why _____

Test number six.

You are a bartender and your customer is explaining in a slow logical manner the "step-by-step" procedure to mix their drink and they really have just some of the facts but think they have it right.

What type of communicator is this customer ____
Why _____

Test number seven.

You sell cell phones and cell phone service in the mall. The customer you are presenting to is explaining everything you just said to someone on their phone and then you hear them ask the person on the phone, "How do you feel about this deal?"

What type of communicator is this customer ____
Why _____

Test number eight.

You are on a cold-call representing a software company. After introductions with your prospect along with receiving a strong handshake, you offer a glossy handsome brochure to your prospect. Your prospect comments, "What should I be looking at? Just tell me the key points," with a strong voice.

What type of communicator is this customer ____
Why _____

Test number nine.

You are a server at a restaurant and your patron is eager to engage you in conversation about everything, not just what is on the menu. Their excitement about the specials of the day, along with their comments is nice but you want to take care of business.

What type of communicator is this customer ____
Why _____

Test number ten.

You are a ticket agent at the departing gate at the airport. The arriving flight is delayed for an hour; you announced that information over the speaker system along with a statement that you will call up passengers to the counter if they need to change connecting flights, because that very same airliner is supposed to take the waiting passengers at that gate to another city.

Now you have a passenger approach your counter before anyone was called and you instruct that customer to wait a minute please. They wait what they think is a minute and just walk forward and ask, "Do you have the details for my flight because I need to make phone calls now," you respond, "May I have your boarding pass?" The customer answers, "Here and as you can see I have planned and organized this trip months ago." The customer is looking you directly in the eyes and asking you what is the challenge and that he can figure-out any issues or obstacles, let him assist in the lead.

What two types of communicator is this customer ____
Why _____

The answers to the test.

Test one: answer is *I,* Why: The patron's greet was enthusiastic and could talk about anything.

Test two: answer is *C,* Why: Medical Doctors are trained to be critical thinkers.

Test three: answer is *D,* Why: Fast pace speech, strong tone, demanding now

Test four: answer is *S,* Why: Pleasant, very good listener, assurance for change

Test five: answer is *C,* Why: Very detailed, very organized

Test six: answer is *S,* Why: Step by Step, review mixture, slow, logical

Test seven: answer is *S,* Why: Assurance, feelings

Test eight: answer is *D,* Why: Strong handshake, direct gestures, key points

Test nine: answer is *I,* Why: Engaging, conversationalist, friendly, excited about choices, story telling

Test ten: answer is *DC,* Why: Direct with conversation, impatient, little to no regard for feelings, concern with details, very organized, direct eye contact, looking for challenges, problem solving.

Work Book
Section One of Two

Your assignment here is to review the scenario and write out your sales script applying the "trigger words".

You are selling car and truck tires along with mechanical repairs. A customer comes into the store and spends a few minutes looking around. You approach them and inquirer about their needs. With a big smile and a warm greeting you both begin to have a dialogue.

What type of communicator is this customer ____ Write your sales dialogue here:

_____

_____

You are selling a service over the phone with your customer base requesting your calls. You make the call the prospect answers the phone and you say, "Good morning this is Madison, is this Mr. Dylan?" the response back in a polite evenly pace tone of voice is, "Yes, I am Dylan and where are you calling me from?" "The medical insurance company ABC has me calling you because you have some more questions, that I will be happy to answer" Mr. Dylan, "Oh yes, I need a few more facts about the coverage, please."

What type of communicator is this customer ____ Write your sales dialogue here:

_____

_____

You are selling car parts over the phone and in your business selling model you have both in-bound and out-bound calls. You answer the phone the customer said, "I need a door for a F150, do you have it?" with a strong demanding voice. Your response is, "I need more information to select the correct door." "What do you need to know?" is the quick response.

What type of communicator is this customer ____ Write your sales dialogue here:

_____

_____

You are selling a very powerful software program that is design to handle all the purchasing needs for corporation from seven figures to a billion dollars a year. The selling cycle is typically several months or meetings. You are now going to perform a scheduled follow-up call to one of three persons and which each person is representing a different department that is involved with the purchase.

You call and the phone is answered. You say, "This is Jacob with 123 and I am calling for Mia," the receptionist response is, "Jacob, Mia is expecting your call, I will put you through now." You hear in a direct but thoughtful with little modulation in the voice, "Hello, this is Mia," your answer is, "I have the updates for you this morning are you ready for them?" Mia with a slow and methodical answer said, "Yes, providing you have better analysis with documentation available".

What type of communicator is the customer ____ What type of communicator is the caller _____
Write your sales dialogue here:

_____

_____

_____

_____

Work Book
Section Two of Two

Your assignment here is to review the scenario and write out your sales script applying the "trigger words".

Test one, section two.

You are an outside Commercial Account salesperson for a cable company offering a suite of products and today you are making a B2B cold call. No schedule appointment, you're tired of hearing your prospect tell you they don't have enough time right now.

You pull into the driveway of the business with your vehicle nicely cleaned. First before you exit your vehicle you look-around and notice the parking lot and the building are pristine. Now you are walking towards the office and "WOW" you think because of the landscaping. As you enter the building it has a marble entrance with a directory of business and which floor they are on. You find the company, a hotel chain's corporate office and now you are in the elevator going to the fifth floor.

What type of communicator would demand this presentation for their corporate offices? _____ Once in the office the business dressed receptionist greets you and you say, "_____
_____.".

Test two, section two.

You are the owner/operator of a gym and health spa. You are experiencing more highs and lows in your membership then what is typical for your market and you need to established predictable sustainability. On this day you are involved with sales and your first prospect is in one of the sales offices.

"Hey, my name is Hailey and I am the owner of Under the Oaks gym and health spa and let's talk about you,"

"My name is Noah and I am twenty-eight and the fact is I need to get in shape and your gym seems like everyone gets along better good here". Hailey answers, "I am happy you feel that way," and "Let's review and I need you to work with me because we have a tailored program for you but first tell me which is most important to you, results now or a fun workout or a step by step process or a proven old school workout?"

Noah is a _____ communicator. Why? _____

_____

Test three, section three.

You work for a family business; your father Christopher (step-by-step) and your uncle Andrew (details and more details) own a health supplement business with the number one protein drink in the Americas. You, Cody (the fun guy) are the sales manager with the task of hiring professional sales persons. There is a job description (your sister Gracie, HR department, need results now) which outlines the responsibilities but your experience is that the definition of words somehow changes depending on the person character or communication strengths.

So you outline the most important duties that are need to be completed with that job and then to find the person that enjoys doing those task naturally. The process of weighing out which is the most important is a Herculaneum task because they are all important.

The first on the list is "closer" need to be a closer, need to be "fun", need to "patient" and stick to the facts and must be good with reports because of the "detail".

Now you are ready for the first interview. You have everything prioritized, the talents along with the skill set needed and Gracie agrees that you are not just going hire them and fire who doesn't work out.

The candidate has all the proper paperwork and let the interview begin. You say, "Hi Fallyn, my name is Cody and I will be conducting your interview today, I am the Sales Manager here also," Fallyn responds, "Hi Cody, I have used all the products from American Superior Nutrition and the fact is they all work great!"

"Thank you Fallyn for being a very good customer and that endorsement," said Cody. "You're welcome," in a pleasant polite voice is what you heard

and you have learned that Fallyn is a _____ type communicator.
Which translates that _____ are important and so are the
_____. But being a strong _____ is possible if the
_____ are strong.

However you understand that there will probably be less drama if she is a
high scoring letter _____.
If the position demands someone who will bring a lot of excitement to the sales
and marketing department then an _____ type communicator
is needed.

Should the position need a self-started and problem solver that gets it done for
a bonus, and does not take issues personally then you need a _____
type communicator?

Details, data and more details along with analysis that ensures accuracy
and that person is thoughtful then you need a _____ type
communicator.

Talk with Larry Wood at: www.SalesDominator.net